espresso shots
& forget-me-nots

selected poems

espresso shots
& forget-me-nots

selected poems
parker lee

ESPRESSO SHOTS & FORGET-ME-NOTS: SELECTED
POEMS

Editor: amanda lovelace
www.amandalovelace.com

Cover and Interior Formatting: Parker Lee
www.byparkerlee.com

Cover Artwork: Ben Eshleman
www.beneshleman.com

The Fell Types are digitally reproduced by Igino Marini.
www.iginomarini.com

ISBN: 9798857921425

Content Warning

espresso shots & forget-me-nots contains sensitive material relating to the following topics:

abandonment, alcohol use, cheating, death, gender dysphoria, queerphobia, toxic relationships, and potentially more.

Please remember to practice self-care before, during, and after reading.

*for everyone
who stood by me
as i practiced the art
of becoming.*

Foreword by amanda lovelace

in a literal sense, this book is a collection of (mostly) previously published poems by my spouse, parker lee, but as i was reading it for the first time, i couldn't help but to think that, in a poetic sense, it would be more accurately described as *a collection of memories*.

ones that taste like plain, bitter espresso.

ones that smell ever-so-softly of forget-me-nots.

ones that are somehow both at the same time—forget-me-not infused espresso, if you will.

while there might be some disagreement on what constitutes as poetry, one thing i think most of us can agree on is that it awakens something deep within the soul of its readers. it might make you feel moved. it might make you feel sad or angry or empowered. it might make you feel understood for the very first time. sometimes it can even amuse you.

as you settle in to read *espresso shots & forget-me-nots*, you can expect to feel the full range of emotions that makes modern poetry so sought-after. within these one-hundred-something pages, parker has refined their already-breathtaking words (& added some new ones) & captured exactly what it's like to be so delicately, frustratingly, & complicatedly human.

laced with love,
amanda

Dear Reader,

In early 2016, I fell in love—with something called *poetry*. Even though writing, creating, and storytelling were things I already enjoyed doing in different forms, outside of the very rare rhymey love poem, I never really wrote much poetry—that is, until there was an aligning-of-the-stars moment for me. In the spring of 2016, I took my first creative writing class, and about halfway into the semester, we shifted from writing fiction and short stories to writing poetry. It was such an eye-opening experience because we were encouraged to step outside of traditional forms and rhyme schemes and experiment with free verse. It showed me that poetry was so much more than I had ever thought it could be.

Around the same time, my then-fiancée (now-wife), amanda, had been giving me modern poetry recommendations to read, which introduced me to additional styles of poetry that differed from what I was reading in class. amanda also told me they were almost finished writing a poetry collection that they intended to self-publish. That book was titled *the princess saves herself in this one*, which went on to win the 2016 Goodreads Choice Award for Best Poetry before being traditionally published in 2017. I was—above all else—proud of amanda, but I was also very inspired.

That inspiration, combined with my newfound love of poetry, led me to writing poems in a little blue journal with the intent of compiling them into my own collection of poems. I wrote whenever and wherever I could—in my car during my breaks at work, in the student lounge between classes at college, at home, at the park. There was a hunger for words, and getting absolutely everything I had ever felt onto paper. I eventually finished my first manuscript, titled *DROPKICKpoetry*, and, well ... it wasn't great. The book felt very disjointed because I tried to touch on too many topics and didn't yet have the skill to weave them together seamlessly. After talking to amanda about my concerns, we both agreed it might be better if I narrowed the focus down to just a topic or two. Following our conversation, I cut everything but a single section from that mess of a manuscript and expanded it into its own book. And thus, my debut poetry collection, *DROPKICKromance* (*2018*), was born.

My second book, *masquerade* (*2019*), was in many ways the debut collection I initially tried to write. The structure was very similar to what I attempted back then, and I even pulled some poems and ideas directly out of the *DROPKICKpoetry* manuscript for *masquerade*. When I finished writing it, I felt that *masquerade* was my *Magnum Opus*—or *Great Work*. Within those pages, I had finally found *my* voice, and not only did it contain some of my strongest poetry, it also contained poems relating to my struggle with my gender identity and the discovery and acceptance of myself as a non-binary person. While some of those poems originally came from that scrapped *DROPKICKpoetry* manuscript, this was the first time anyone else but me would be reading them, so it was an important moment for me on a personal level. It also felt important because I hoped to use the small platform I was privileged enough to have to be the representation I so desperately needed when I was a kid.

After getting the rights back to both *DROPKICKromance* and *masquerade* in October of 2022, I spent a lot of time trying to figure out what I wanted to do with them. I knew I didn't want to simply re-release the books as they were, but I also couldn't figure out how I wanted to bring them back. Though I experimented with a few different ideas, I never felt passionate about any of them. That is, until I realized that even though these books existed as separate, sister titles, they both were birthed from the same place—the scrapped *DROPKICKpoetry* manuscript. I wanted whatever I did with both to honor my previous work *and* celebrate my growth as a writer. What better way to do that than to bring the two books back together as one and finally create the book I had initially intended to write?

Putting this book together was like assembling a puzzle—I had almost all the pieces, so it was only a matter of putting them in place and filling in the gaps. The collection you hold in your hands now is a collection consisting of poems you might know from my previously published works, as well as some new and previously unpublished poems, pieced together to form one complete story—mine. It's a story of love, heartbreak, and learning to love again. It's a story of both losing yourself and finding yourself. It's a story of self-discovery and growth. It's a story about realizing your worth and taking back your personal power. It's a story about painting yourself with starlight and proudly being the most authentic version of yourself.

Whether you've been around since the very beginning of my journey or this book is your first introduction to my work, I just wanted to say thank you. Thank you for being here, for giving me a chance, and for letting my words in. This book holds a special place in my heart, and I hope it finds a home in yours, too.

With love,
Parker

espresso shots & forget-me-nots

the espresso machine has been collecting dust.
coffee beans have grown stale in the grinder's hopper,
and a sprig of forget-me-nots has made a home
inside the cortado glass resting on the countertop.
sometimes, it's almost too easy to forget about
what was once a part of your everyday life,

to let memories dissipate into thin air, like steam
rolling off the mouth of a too-hot cup of coffee.
but there is beauty in both remembering and forgetting.
some memories are too meaningful to let wither away.
some memories are too bitter to be worth remembering,
and some memories are worth preserving even if they are.

so this is me cleaning out the espresso machine,
this is me pouring fresh coffee beans in the hopper,
this is me washing the cortado glass and pressing
the forget-me-nots between pages of old poetry,
this is me sipping on something that is both
a little bit bitter and a little bit sweet.

PART I

innocence

whatever happened to the one
whose hands could put pencil to paper
and turn imagination into reality?
whose feet could step out the backyard door
and into another world?
the one with eyes ready to swallow the sky whole
and a heart ambitious enough to do it?

whatever happened to the one
who raced from dawn 'til dusk,
waving in the wind on wings of wax
to wrap their fingertips around the sun,
yet ran from the glow of streetlights?
the one who decided even the sun wasn't enough
and pocketed entire galaxies instead?

whatever happened to the one
whose dreams were so grand
the universe itself had to expand
to keep up the pace?
the one who refused to be contained
and became a universe themself?
the one you're thinking about right now?

skull kid

childhood is the time
that one reaches
toward the sky
and grows into the person
they were meant to be.
but for me,

childhood was the time
that i reached
toward fictional faces
and buried my roots
within a flawless
facade.

childhood was the time
that i rejected
my own growth to mirror
the growth of others because
i wasn't sure who i was
supposed to be.

chameleon

i exist somewhere between fact and fiction—
one who has worn many masks of many shades,

one who has said things they never should have said,
done things they never should have done,

became someone they never should have became,
all in the name of blending in with their surroundings.

stained glass mirror

sometimes
you want so desperately
to please everybody
that you chip off a piece
of those you meet
and stick them together,
turning yourself into
a mosaic of everything
you think
they want you to be—
but when you break yourself down
into such tiny pieces,
there's never quite enough
of any one thing
to keep them satisfied.

the masked magician

i have learned that some people
will take the magic from their
palms and place it in yours,
and as soon as you learn
how to make your own,
they'll try to take credit
for what now flows through
every fiber of your being.
but that magic was already
inside of you, and just because
they showed you it exists,
doesn't make it theirs to wield.

misplaced

i used to be a piece of a puzzle
lost in the box of another.
no matter where i was placed,
or which way i was turned,
there wasn't space for me
in the big picture. eventually,
i got tired of trying to fit into
someplace i didn't belong.

can't hurt what you can't see

i stay quiet
because when
you're quiet,
nobody pays you
any mind.

i keep to myself
because when
you keep to yourself,
you can't step
on anyone's toes.

i make myself invisible
because when
you're invisible,
everybody looks
right through you.

mirror, mirror

a child stands in front of a mirror,
dissecting their own reflection
with scalpel-like precision.

why was i born into this body?
why can't i change what i was given?
why don't i get a say in who i am?

the mirror doesn't answer, doesn't offer any
insight into the truth, because there is no
magic here, just a man-made construct.

cracks in the glass

every time i try to make sense
of the disconnect between
how i look
on the outside
and how i feel
on the inside,
i am interrupted
by a voice that only
repeats the same line:

you are broken.
you are broken.
you are broken.

and that is all it takes
to send me back within myself,
to make me deny every single question
i've ever been bold enough
to ask about myself.

if i am broken,
then so be it, but nobody
will ever know
how broken i am.

trust issues

locking up my thoughts
and feelings eventually
became a thing of habit.

too many people
pushed me away
without ever giving me
a chance.

too many friends
turned their backs
without ever giving me
an explanation.

it's not that trust
is something i am
incapable of giving,

but rather it is my most
prized possession,
one i could never part with

unless i found someone
i knew was worth
sharing it with.

death's-head

when this caterpillar emerged from its cocoon,
it didn't have the prismatic wings of a butterfly
but ones as black as night, marked in the center
with a skull-shaped warning: *don't get too close.*

long distance lover

we admire the beauty of the stars from afar because we know
that to touch one would mean to get burned, and i think i fall
in love the very same way.

unsuspecting

the thing about
keeping the world
at arm's length
is that it becomes

far too easy
to become attached
to the first person who shows you
the slightest bit of affection.

a web of hopeless romantics

we have the entire world
at our fingertips,
so why should we limit ourselves
to only what's right in front of us?

when words
are the only interaction
you have with someone,
you have no choice

but to get to know them
for what's on the inside,
so how can this be
any less real?

hopelessly hopeless

once there was a person who spent years clinging to a relationship that was more heartache than love, who couldn't be pushed away even by countless lies and infidelities. some might say that they were a hopeless romantic grasping to the idea that true love could conquer anything, but when you fall in love with an idea of who a person *could* be instead of who they *really* are, then it isn't true love, and it isn't romantic— it's just hopeless.

screaming infidelities

few things are more delicate than trust,

and even fewer are the ways

it can be destroyed so completely

than by a partner who takes your heart

and slow dances on it with another behind

your back. it's something that fundamentally

changes who you are because from that moment

on, there is only who you were *before*

and who you are *after*. yes, there is pain,

and yes, it hurts, but it eventually fades.

what's lingers is the doubt—the doubt

that keeps you searching for double

meanings in every word. the doubt

that keeps you questioning every single

interaction between them and another.

the doubt that keeps you looking

for betrayals that might not actually exist,

but wouldn't surprise you if they did.

the betrayals that do exist, and do surprise

you, even though you know they shouldn't.

the details you think you would've been

better off not knowing, even though

knowing is always better than being

left in the dark. the little things that

start the cycle of doubt all over again.

intrusive thoughts

who is that?

how do you know them?

do you two talk a lot?

hang out a lot?

have you told them about me?

why haven't you told them about me?

how to trick yourself into coping with trust issues:

"promise?"

mixtape

i survived a romance that would make even a mixtape of the saddest emo songs about the most toxic relationships shed a tear. the type of romance that leaves you addicted to the high of feeling low. the type of romance that convinces you that you'll never make it on your own even though that's all you've ever really known. the type of romance where the act of them finally leaving you is really a heartbreak-wrapped gift, because you were far too lost to ever find the way out on your own.

origami sky

i spent the winter in my basement
picking up memories in the form
of multicolored squares folded
into the shapes of cranes and puffy
little stars, enough to fill a galaxy.
i took a moment to admire
every crease and the way
something so intricate could be made
from something so simple.

but it's so sad, isn't it?

to know that no matter how much time
you put into creating something beautiful,
it takes only a moment to destroy it—
to squeeze a star between your fingertips
until its light flickers and dies.
to lift a crane up by its wings
and gently pull them apart until
the tension becomes too much
and it tears in two.

eternal sunshine

sometimes you have to

tear up the photos,

burn the letters,

and scrub their fingerprints

from your skin.

sometimes you have to

delete their number,

wipe them from your memory,

and forget they ever

e x i s t e d .

tiny pockets of moving on

and then one day,
they are not the first person you text
when you wake up in the morning.

hard to love

i made myself into a martyr of love
because it was easier than admitting
i was not always an easy person to be with.
my expectations were too high and i demanded
a lot. i was tired of feeling like a runner up
in my own relationships, and desperation
is rarely a good look on anybody.
that isn't to say i deserved to have my trust
broken so many times that the pieces
became too tiny to pick up—because i didn't—
but in being forced to rebuild myself,
i learned how to love in a way that is
a little less jagged, and a lot more gentle.

naïve

young love is a beautifully dangerous
thing because it's so pure but such
an easy thing to lose yourself in.
it can be all-consuming, taking over
every spare thought, word, and second
of your life until it's the only thing
you know how to define yourself by.
when it's gone, so is any semblance
of who it is you used to be.

costume change

i became an expert
at hiding myself
behind masks,
but it turns out there wasn't
one big enough or
convincing enough
to hide this heartbreak,
so i became someone
else entirely.

fixer-upper

self-confidence is built in layers,
but there isn't one *right* way to do it.

sometimes it starts from the inside out
as you learn to love the person you are today.

sometimes it starts from the outside in
as you project the person you hope to one day become.

sometimes you even have to tear yourself down
to the bones and rebuild everything from the ground up.

in the midwest, meijer is the only place to go

every day,
i drove to the same lot.

every day,
i parked in the same spot.

every day,
i listened to the same sad songs.

every day,
i simply existed.

it was
the only thing i knew how to do.

if love wants me, it knows where to find me

i'd always thought that love
was something to be chased,
something i had to be
in relentless pursuit of,

but, over time, i found that
to chase love
is to chase heartbreak,
and i haven't a heart
left to break.

never say never

i told myself that
i would never love again.

i told myself that
there wasn't anyone else
out there for me,
and even if there was,

i told myself that
it didn't matter.

[i was wrong, there was, and it did.]

spring's first thaw

the moment it happened
is difficult to pinpoint,
but as if all at once,

there was no longer
a *before*, or an *after*—
there was only
you.

PART II

twin souls

how could it be
that your soul and mine
fit together so completely?

i travel light-years in keystrokes

we talked
from dawn to dusk,
thousands of messages
traveling between our fingertips
at lightning speed,
and never once
did we run out of things
to say.

unburden

tell me everything.
take the weight of the world
off your weary shoulders
and let me carry it on mine,
because you've been
burdened by it
for far too long.

parking lots of broken hearts

little did i know,
while i was off hiding
in parking spaces
and piecing myself
back together,
you were doing
the very same thing
hundreds of miles away.

parker lee

pleasantville

my life had become
devoid of color,
but then you came into it,

and every lost hue—
even ones i had never
seen before—
returned

one

by

one

by

one

like cherry blossoms
b u r s t i n g
to   life
in   the   spring,

brighter
and more vivid
than ever.

i knew i could trust you from the moment i met you

there was just
something about you.
without a word,
you managed to
piece together
what had been
meticulously
picked apart and
put on display
for all to see.

without a word,
you showed me
a heart that knew
what it was like
to have its trust
s h a t t e r e d,
a heart without
the capability of
doing the same
to another.

from the broken we'll make art

we found each other
a jagged mess of every color
the universe had ever thought up.

old loves shaped us,
shattered us,
and left us
to pick up the pieces.

and so
we pieced each other
back together,

your pieces mixed with mine
and mine mixed with yours
to make the most beautiful
mosaic of love and survival.

the sun has nothing on you

we found each other
in darkness
and made our own light.
together, we burned
brighter than anything
that awaited us
on the other side.

word devourer

you bought me a copy
of your favorite book, and
i ate each word up like candy—
devouring chapter after chapter
until i reached the end,
left hungry
for more.

reading became
my favorite pastime—

with every turn of the page,
with every new chapter,
i got to fall in love
with the same words,
with the same characters,
with the same places
that you fell in love with,

and each time, it was like falling
in love with you all over again.

in every book i read, i see you

i see you
in every heroine
who isn't afraid
to stand up and say whatever's on their mind.

i see you
in every heroine
who wears the term "unlikable"
like a badge of honor.

i see you
in every heroine
who's had to endure the unimaginable
yet still finds the strength to fight another day.

i see you
in every heroine
who's had to carry a revolution
she never asked to be part of in the first place.

big bang theory

we had the makings
of star-crossed lovers,
but we fought our way
across solar systems,
leaving new planets
in our wake
as the pull of
our shooting-star hearts
formed a galaxy
all their own.

the first cup

i sat at your kitchen table
and watched you brew
us a big pot of coffee, and
when you filled my mug,

you did it the very same way
you filled my heart:

completely oblivious
to just how vital
either would become
to my everyday life.

like leaves, we're falling

you and me,
the sun peeking through
the flame-topped trees,
windows cracked,
that song about
autumn gold
filling the calm
around us.

you and me,
fingers laced,
your hand
squeezing gently
like a pulse,
a sign that we
couldn't be more alive
than we are in this moment.

favorite places

we packed a picnic
and you whisked me away
to your favorite place,

where we ate sandwiches
on everything bagels,
drank pumpkin spice coffee,

took pictures with our faces
hidden behind our favorite book,
and got lost in each other.

autumn has nothing on you

i picked up
the single red leaf
lying atop the
hueless remains
of those that had
fallen before it,
held it up to the sky

like a flickering flame
against a tidal wave,
and i looked at you and said,
"i have yet to find
a single thing
as vibrant
as you."

vernal equinox

in the spring,
you showed me
what it was
to live.

autumnal equinox

in the autumn,
you showed me
what it was
to be alive.

october soulmates

october:
birth and rebirth,
steaming cups of coffee,
treetops ignited above us
like newly stricken matchsticks.
"just like your hair," you said,

then you called me
your "october love"
and i became determined
more than ever before
to be someone worthy
of the name.

this is not goodbye

i placed my heart in your palm
and wrapped your fingers around it
the way i wrapped my scarf
around your neck
when you said it was too cold,
and kissed the back
of your hand—

a promise
that this was only temporary.
a promise
that i would be back.
a promise
that, no matter what,
i am yours.

EWR –> DTW

i sat in terminal b
of newark international
hiding tears behind
big sunglasses.

leaving you
was the last thing
i ever wanted
to do,

but gorgeous,
i swear to you
i'll be back
before you know it.

perfect strangers

my father picked me up from the airport
and the only thing we managed to talk
about was how the new jersey weather
compared to the weather in michigan.

neither one of us had been known
for being an open book, but still the conversation
was stilted and jarring, like two strangers

making small talk in a coffee shop line
rather than parent and child of 25 years.
i was the one who had just gotten off an airplane,
but he was the one somewhere else entirely.

skype date

i could see your face
and hear your voice,
but what i wouldn't give
to reach through this screen.
now that i've
known your touch,
there's no living
without it.

coffee cup romance

the only thing i could do
to fill the void
the distance left me with
was to cling to the clothes
that still carried your scent
and take my coffee
the same way you take yours.
(i think it just made me miss you
more.)

lonely ≠ alone

i look out
the backseat window

of a car filled
with all of my

best friends
and rest my eyes

on the moon,
wondering:

how can it be that the moon is
surrounded by all of the stars

in the nighttime sky
and still it looks so

lonely?

homeward bound

time
is the
achilles' heel
of distance;
with enough of it,
no distance
is too great
to overcome.

a new chapter

i am up before the sun,
cramming as much of
the last twenty-five years
into a four-door sedan
as i can. we said our farewells
the night before because we
knew it would be too hard.
and while leaving behind
the only family and the only home
i've ever known is one of the most
difficult things i have ever done,
it is also one of the easiest,
knowing that you're waiting
for me at the end of the journey.

my forever destination

we crashed into each other's arms
as if another second apart
would've killed us,
and it was then that i made
a silent vow—
a promise
to never again
let the miles
stand between us.

stealing seconds

waking up early just
to stop by your house
for the few moments
it took us to have our
morning coffee.

a natural progression

morning coffee turned into
after-work coffee,
which turned into
before-bed coffee,
which turned into
a mug in your cupboard,
a toothbrush in your bathroom,
and three totes full of my belongings
in the spare bedroom.

your passion is my passion

i could spend eternity
following you around
every corner
of every bookstore,
watching you search for
the perfect story
to get lost in.

august 15th, 2015

i carved out a hole in the center
of our favorite book
and tucked my heart
inside of it.

i led you to
the wooden fairytale bridge
overlooking the river
and dropped to a knee.

looking into your eyes,
i opened to the bookmarked page
and asked the most important question
that would ever pass through these lips.

storybook romance

let's build bookshelves together
and fill them with our story
because ours will always be
my favorite.

muse

you gave me books
and showed me
how to live
a thousand and one lives.

you gave me a pen
and inspired me
to write
this one.

laced with love

you are the only one who can say my name
and put out fires rather than start them.

the countdown

i've always had
a bad perception
of time, so it wasn't
until our wedding
was two weeks
away that it finally
started to feel real.
two weeks until
you walk down
the aisle at our
favorite place,
in front of all our
favorite people,
during our
favorite season,
on the five year
anniversary of
the moment i asked
you to be
forever with me.
two weeks until
we recite love
poems, take each
other by the hand,
and make a vow
to stand by each
other's side until
the clock runs out.

october 13ᵗʰ, 2017

she walked out from beneath the canopy
with autumn wrapped around their body
and twilight courting night in her hair.
the sun, moon, and stars trailed behind,
taking in the light only they could give.

the cove

we got the keys to an empty
one-bedroom apartment
with bright white walls
and bare hardwood floors,
and when you set your
bag on the floor,
all i could think about was
how much potential there was
to make this little space our own.
we could line the walls with bookshelves,
and make our first memories
as newlyweds.
we could create a life of poetry—
not just on paper,
but in the living, breathing
sense of the word.

no roots

home is an apartment where we eat pizza on cardboard boxes before we have our own table to sit at, but it's also a five-hour car ride through winding roads as the sun first peeks over the hilltops. it's the airports, train stations, taxis, and hotel rooms. it's a bench beside a pond in a new jersey park, and a covered bridge spanning a river in a tiny michigan village. it's the bookstores, coffee shops, and every single aisle in target. home is anywhere i have left my footprints beside yours.

sun, rain & soil
after amanda lovelace

she says flowers grow
wherever my fingertips graze,
but every bud bursting from beneath
the surface is because she dared
blossom despite those who thought
her petals were theirs for the picking.

5:30 am

some might think
i envy the mug
that touches your lips
in the early morning,
but what i actually envy
is the first sip of coffee
that wraps around your soul
like a hug and helps you get through
even the toughest of days.

full circle moments

we used to sit alone
in different parking lots
hundreds of miles away—
listening to music,
simply existing,
and mending the pieces
of our broken hearts.

now we sit together
in the same parking lot,
inches from each other—
listening to music
and simply existing
because those hearts
are now overflowing with love.

you are living, breathing poetry

it's easy
to turn the hurt
into poetry.

hurt is ugly—
it doesn't need
to be wrapped in a bow
or buried beneath a bed of roses.

turning the good
into poetry
is much more difficult.

fully capturing the way
you glance at me out of the corner of your eye
when you know i'm gazing at you
as if seeing an autumn sunset
for the first time—

the way
your legs get tangled with mine underneath the table
at our favorite coffee shop
as we spill our hearts
into word documents—

the way
our pinkies search for one another
as we walk side by side
at our favorite park,
interlocking as they meet—

is an impossibility,
because even though these moments
have more meaning behind them
than if we reached into the sky
and wrote our names amongst the stars,

they are already poetry
in its rawest form.
attempting to put them into words,
no matter how flowery they are,

is like translating
from one language
to another,
something always
getting lost in translation.

water witch

it's a rainy september morning,
and autumn brushes her lips gently
against our skin for the first time
this year, and it's like every poem
i've ever written about us—you
and me sitting in our favorite café,
sipping on cups of pumpkin spice,
legs tangled beneath the table, but now,
in the moments between stanzas,
i absentmindedly reach for the ring
you slid onto my finger last october.
now, there is an apartment for us
to return to, but only for another month
because soon we'll be packing up
everything we've collected over the years
and moving it all into a house of our very own,
with a window perch for our cat and a tiny
deck in the back for drinking coffee
and watching the yellows, reds, and oranges
dance in the wind in celebration of the new
life we've built for ourselves.

october is for lovers

october is for first dates and wedding days.

october is for steaming carryout cups before photos in the pick-your-own pumpkin patch.

october is for chilly apple orchard adventures and warming up with cups of hot cider.

october is for scenic fall foliage drives and sitting underneath the most colorful tree.

october is for crunching leaves beneath our feet as we walk side-by-side along the breezy coastline.

october is for fiery flower crowns on our heads and purple asters in our garden bed.

october is for new beginning after new beginning, but never forgetting how far we've come.

october is for lovers, because october was made for you and me.

the only one

with you, there is no pretending.
you see me like nobody sees me.
you know me like nobody knows me.
you accept me like nobody accepts me.

PART III

lost and found

i have discovered that it is possible
to find yourself and lose yourself
at the exact same time.

october 25th, 2016

i have been me for twenty-nine years,
and i still don't know what that means.

graverobber

my mouth has become a cemetery
lined with the headstones of every word

that has died on my tongue while
attempting to escape my spiderweb-throat.

i've tried digging up the corpses,
piecing their bones back together

and spitting out their skeletons, but
i kept choking on the graveyard dirt,

so i had a few drinks to make it easier.
the first to wash down the soil,

the second to burn away the threads,
and the third to find the courage

to wrap my lips around the words
that would set me free from the tomb

i've been trapped inside
from the moment i was conceived.

the flood

i don't know how to explain it other than as a dam bursting. i had spent a lifetime time building walls inside of myself to contain feelings i could never properly articulate, feelings that left a teenage me thinking they were broken, but it only took a single drunken night to crack the surface and unleash a flood of repression all at once. it took time to navigate the waters, to wade through the debris of what my reality used to be, and what i have now discovered about myself. it's like knowing everything and knowing nothing all at the same time, but at least now, my gender dysphoria has a name. at least now, i no longer have to masquerade as someone i never really was. at least now, i am free to be me, whoever that may be.

linked

imagine wearing a mask for so long
that the skin beneath learns its shape
and begins tracing its edges, blurring
the lines between person and persona.

imagine the searing realization when
you try tearing it off for the first time,
and see just how much of your life
you have allowed this act to become.

imagine the patience and the precision
needed to delicately sever the bond
and pull the skin away from the mask
to remove the facade from the flesh.

imagine the confusion when you see
yourself for the first time without it,
and the face looking back at you is one
you no longer recognize as your own.

dysphoria i

sometimes
i look at others
and wonder
if i'd be more
comfortable in my
skin if i wore
theirs
instead.

dysphoria ii

would you
mind if we
traded places
and i lived inside
your body
for a while?
mine has become
a cage.

hate/hate relationship

some days, i hate my body for what it is.
other days, i hate my body for what it isn't.

binary breaker

i dream of deconstruction, breaking
myself down to the cellular level,
analyzing my genetic material,
tinkering with my chromosomes,
following my own set of blueprints.

i dream of reconstruction, building
myself back up to the human form,
watching myself become the person
on the outside that has been screaming
from the inside for anyone to hear.

the alchemy of me

i think back to the version of me
who figured out how to transmute
self-doubt into self-confidence,

and i wonder if they'd be proud
of the mess i have become—
the person who struggles

to make eye contact
with their own reflection,
the person who craves acceptance

but still keeps the world
at arm's length. it's true
that i've figured out

something about myself
that even they wouldn't
let themself piece together,

but is that enough?
am i enough?
will i ever learn

how to turn water
into wine?
lead into gold?

the collector

every time i peel back another layer, every time i feel like i've
finally gotten to the very core of who i am, i find that i've still
done little more than scratch the surface. so i peel, and i peel,
and i peel, and i peel, and i peel, and i begin wondering if i
even really exist or if i'm just a collection of everything i'd
hoped to be but never became.

october 25th, 2017

i don't know how much longer
i can stay in a body
that's never felt like home,
in a mind that knows the problem
and the solution, but is too afraid
to let me solve it,
or in a life
where a glass of whiskey
holds more truth
than my own honest heart
ever has.

smokey eye

eyeliner as defiance.
eyeliner as a statement,
a declaration, a *fuck you*
to a society that shames
people for expressing
themselves the way they
feel the most at home,
the same society that labels
everything from toys to
toothbrushes "boy" and "girl"
rather than letting individuals
cultivate their own identities.

eyeliner as a call to arms.
eyeliner as a weapon,
a raised fist, a shield
from judgmental expressions
and microaggressions
disguised as questions,
from the insults and slurs
shot out of car windows
like bullets in a drive-by
because i dare exist
in a way they don't
and refuse to understand.

eye contact

it's springtime in the city
and i'm sitting outside the strand
waiting for my favorite poet to take
stage and make some kind of magic.
i fiddle with my sunglasses, my eyes
a smudgy, smokey mess. i've gotten
better at blending the pigment,

but i'm still not great at it
and nowhere near as confident
as i was before i stopped wearing it.
coming back to yourself is never easy
when you've masqueraded as someone else
for so long. you have to relearn how to walk
in your own boots and speak with your own

tongue because it's forgotten the shape
of truth. it's a process of unbecoming
and becoming again, a process
that can wait until tomorrow.
i begin to slide my sunglasses back
up the bridge of my nose like i'm
slipping into a second suit of armor,

when i make eye contact with a woman
who stops midstride before taking a few steps back.
i immediately wish i kept the cis cosplay on today,
expecting to relive the street harassment
of my teenage years, but it never happens.
instead, she smiles and tells me "i like your
makeup" before continuing down broadway.

it's springtime in the city
and i'm sitting outside the strand
waiting for my favorite poet to take
stage and make some kind of magic.
i take off my sunglasses, and hang them
from the collar of my shirt, and i carry
a different kind of magic inside with me.

nyc

the city doesn't care.
it pays no mind and
casts no judgment.

it's here, in this endless
sea of faces, where i feel
most comfortable being me.

october 25th, 2018

it's been months since the word
non-binary set me free—free to
be the most me i have ever been.
and yet, i can't shake the feeling
that while i've become well-versed
in the art of becoming, i still have
a long way to go in perfecting it.

internalized

i think deep down,
i knew who i was
meant to become
from a young age,
but when you lack
the language needed
to describe how you
feel on the inside,
when all you know
about people like you
comes from harmful
tropes and unapologetic
bigotry in the movies
and on the tv screen,
it becomes far too easy
to learn how to hate
yourself without ever
really knowing *why*.
it becomes far too easy
to bury that part of
yourself before they
ever had a chance
to be *alive*.

choke

my name doesn't fit quite
right these days, like a shirt
collar that wraps around
my neck a little too tightly—

not so tight that it stops my
breath, but just enough to
leave me tugging at it every
time it touches my throat.

what's in a name?

my birth name was passed down
to me by my father and to him
by his father. i was the third
of this namesake—the first
has already passed away,
and the second exists as a
memory of what used to be.
but as for me? i am the one
who finally puts an end to it.
my birth name carried the weight
of every mistake they've made,
their deceit disguised as decency.
my birth name was the name
of someone i strived to be like
before realizing they were never
the person i thought they were.
my birth name is living proof
that even the "good men"
can disappoint us in the end.
my birth name is the eulogy
for a person i could never be.

landslide

i remember that day like it was yesterday.
it was a sunday afternoon, december 2nd .
i was off work early, and i knew everyone
was going to be home at the same time.
i was planning on breaking the news that had
me wrestling with my nerves for weeks:
i was not just moving away home, i was leaving
the entire state of michigan 658 miles behind.
however nothing could've prepared me for the
sucker-punch text i got as i punched out of my shift
and walked to my car. i still remember the way the air
was forced from my lungs when i stepped
into our house, the broken hearts of your broken
family, the helplessness that gave way to rage,
the avalanche you left in your wake as you
abandoned the only life you'd known
because you were too much of a coward
to face the consequences of your actions,
and the way you took everything with you
on your way out, leaving us without so much
as a shovel to dig ourselves out with.

fault lines

i kept asking myself if there was something i could've done to change the outcome, if there was something i could've said to make you stay. that's how it always goes when someone leaves, though, isn't it? you think about every interaction you've ever had with them and try to pinpoint the exact moment everything was set into motion, like if you had handled things just a little differently, then maybe, just maybe, everything would be okay—they would still be here, and you wouldn't have this guilt filling the hole their absence left inside of you. but sometimes there's nothing that could've changed what happened. sometimes, a person's place in your life is meant to be temporary. sometimes, it's okay to put the blame on them, where it belongs, rather than on yourself.

unbury

you took so much from us when you walked out the door that day and refused to come back, and i refuse to let you take my future from me. i am still moving on with my life, and maybe it is selfish of me to leave while the aftermath of your actions is still reverberating through every one of us, but if i don't pull myself out of the wreckage now, i may never stop carrying its weight.

impractical magic

i may have become quite the escape artist,
but you mastered the disappearing act.

last rites

it's a strange thing to see your birth name in the body

of your grandfather's obituary as one who has survived

the dead when you had become the family's ghost

long before he ever passed away.

the next mourning

i skipped the funeral and i think
we all knew it was for the best.
how could i be expected to mourn
the man who watched us grovel
at his feet for help while
pretending he didn't already know
all about what you had done to us?
how could i be expected
to come face-to-face with you
for the first time in two years
with an audience of people
who'd already taken your side
even though you were
the one who fucked up?
how could i be expected
to coexist with family
who no longer looked
at me as part of it?

the severed limb of the family tree

two families who couldn't
be more different got together
in silent understanding
and sawed off the branch
that joined them,
leaving it to rot while
carrying on as if it never
existed in the first place.
no more forced smiles.
no more "you should come
visit more often"s or
"remember the time"s.
no more late birthday cards
or awkward gift exchanges.
no more feigned interest
in each other's lives.

like father

i thought i saw you at the pet store once. well, maybe i didn't *really* think it was you, but i did have to do a double take—a triple take, even. i'm not really sure what you look like these days, though i imagine it was close to the man who looked at the cats in his black baseball cap, university-of-michigan-colored satin jacket, light wash blue jeans, and white sneakers. he was a little older than i remember you being, and though a lot can change in six years, there was something so familiar about the way he stood there—a shy smile resting on his lips as he stole glances from those around him, hoping to share a moment with a stranger. *familiar* because i always catch myself looking for acceptance in others the same way.

conflicted

thinking about you
is like walking a tightrope.
i try to keep the balance
between love and hate
because i believe in nuance if nothing else.
while i loved the genuinely good
dad i had for the first twenty-five
years of my life, i cannot stomach
the idea of the man who decided
to remove "father" from his resume
and become nothing but a memory
for the last eleven.

delivered

once in a while
i'll get a text message from you
around my birthday, or on a random holiday,
but i've decided that you don't deserve
a response. you don't deserve
to know if i've even received them.
i have considered changing
the phone number i've had since 2009
a dozen times, not just so you
can't get to me anymore,
but so it isn't entirely a lie if i ever
have to tell you why i never replied.
then i realized that you
just aren't worth the hassle.

reclamation

taking back your power can look
like so many different things,
and for me, it looks like cutting
people out of my life entirely.
it looks like ignored phone calls
and liberal use of the block button.
instead of wasting another ounce
of my energy on people that keep
me from growing, i am putting
everything i have into the ones
who want to see me flourish.

13 things my father missed out on after he left:

1. my last day in michigan
2. meeting the love of my life
3. my first day of college
4. my engagement
5. my wedding
6. my first apartment
7. my first book
8. my college graduation
9. my first house
10. eleven years of birthdays
    (and counting)
11. my second, third,
    and fourth books
12. meeting the person
    i finally found the
    courage to become
13. my respect

spit

i have not seen you
in over a decade, but when
i look at pictures of myself,
or when i brush my teeth
in the morning and catch
my reflection from the wrong
angle, your face meets mine
your eyes
your nose
your jaw
my mouth
my mouth
my. mouth.
i spit into the sink.
i gargle mouthwash.
i spit into the sink again.
i run the water,
and i rinse your name
right down the drain.

scorpio sun

may you one day
find comfort in
the taste of immortality,
for this resentment
will far outlive
either one
of us.

PART IV

tick tock

time is a two-faced mistress
in the way that she both heals
things and destroys them.

i consider my once-broken
heart, healed by the methodical
ticking of the clock's hands.

i consider my soul growing
bitter like an espresso shot left
on the kitchen counter too long.

i consider the lessons both
learned and later forgotten as
our minds transform with age.

i consider all the people that
have come and gone in my life
and wonder who still thinks of me.

better late than never

one problem with me has always been that i waste too much energy looking for the validation of others, when the only validation i've ever needed is my own. it isn't an easy thing to unlearn—bad habits rarely are—but i'm getting better about it. and so will you.

non-linear equations

healing isn't a straight line. some days will always be better than others, and sometimes there might be more bad ones than good ones. tomorrow might see you in bed until late afternoon, fighting to do something as simple as taking a shower, while the next greets you at sunrise with a warm cup of coffee and a to-do list that's finished before noon. never let the bad days make you forget that the good ones are waiting for you across the horizon, just as you are waiting for them.

phases

sometimes i feel as if
the moon shines for me
and me alone.
i look up and marvel
at the way she changes
her masks,
wearing a new face
every single night
but remaining unmistakably
herself. i, too,
have worn many masks,
and only now am i
beginning to understand
that at my very core
i've always been the same.

icarus complex

i want to
spread these wings
and climb to the edge
of the atmosphere.

i want to
feel my breath
forced from my lungs
as the air grows thin.

i want to
hurtle downward
toward the ground
like a shooting star.

just to know that i can.

change

it is mornings like this
when i feel most at peace:
sitting at the kitchen table,
coffee mug in hand,

staring out the window
as sunlight breaks
through blooming branches—
like them, i am blooming, too.

breathe

i am taking in as much life
as my lungs can hold,
and i am learning how to
filter out the toxins

and release the good
back into a world
that so desperately
needs it.

unapologetic

i will not
fit myself into a box
to meet your expectations.

i will not
twist myself into a knot
to earn your appreciation.

the moon's resistance

the sun tells the moon
that her place is at night
with the stars,
but still she hangs
defiantly
in the midafternoon sky,
refusing
to have her place dictated
by another's expectations.

fact #1

the mirror was never meant to be your enemy.

fact #2

beauty isn't always honest,
and the truth isn't always pretty.

fact#3

kindness is not transactional.
never let anyone make you
feel like you're indebted to them
because they showed you the most
basic form of human decency.

charade

beware of those who want you to believe they
have your best interest at heart
while doing everything in their power to shape
you into their image.

bigger

if they tell you to change who you are,
be yourself but even louder.

false hero

too many people
want to speak for others
before speaking for
themselves.

too many people
want to make you better
before bettering
themselves.

too many people
will try to save you
when the one who
truly needs saving

is themselves.

kill grave

some will do whatever it takes
to convince you that they're someone they're not.
they'll speak in half-truths and full lies,
and they'll repeat them as often as it takes
to get you to fall for the trap they've laid.
that's when they'll wrap invisible strings
around your wrists, elbows, ankles, and knees
and make you dance to their old, tired tune.
they'll say everything you want to hear,
break you down just to build you up,
and they'll tell you how you should feel
about it. if you dare question them,
they'll shift the blame and make you
take on every ounce of their guilt.
you might not recognize the warning
signs right away, but when you do,
remember that it was never your fault
for putting your trust in someone
who is incapable of appreciating
the gift you have given them.

stacked

like a magician
whose first language
is sleight of hand,
they give you the
illusion of control—
pick a card, cut
and shuffle the deck
until you're certain
it's well-hidden,
yet somehow they
always know how
to manipulate their
card back to the top.

less is more

apologize less because you have less to apologize for.

highline

i used to think that blowing up bridges was enough to protect me from the people i needed distance from, but that was never the solution. people will find their way to you one way or another, so instead, i am building bigger bridges to better places—places that can only be reached by taking the high road.

terraform

society has a way of bending you until you break, no matter how strong you think you are or how hard you try to fight back. it will try to fold you on top of yourself and shape you into something new—something prettier, smaller. something less you, more them. but it doesn't realize that by doing so, it's creating a warrior out of you, one strong enough to sink mountains and raise tides. strong enough to reach inside the earth and shake it to its very core. strong enough to leave your mark on what's tried to leave a scar on you.

dawn of a new day

the world may reject you today,

but with time comes acceptance.

give it that time, but do not be silent.

let every footstep, every word,

and every breath be an act of resistance.

the world might not be ready for you,

but that doesn't mean you're not ready

to create the tomorrow you deserve.

myth-buster

destroy the idea
that you need to
love yourself
before you can
love someone else
or be loved by them.

self-love
doesn't happen
overnight.

self-love
can be a lifelong
struggle.

self-love
does not dictate
how much love
one deserves,
nor how much
they have to give
to others.

sometimes,
self-love
comes after.

be the one

if they don't believe in you,
then find someone else who does,
even if that someone is yourself.

take

sometimes being a little selfish is the biggest act
of self-love we can give ourselves.

tend to yourself

water the seeds.
tear out the weeds.
feed your new growth.
starve what threatens it.

worthy

love is a wonderful thing,
but it isn't the only wonderful thing.

there is the scent of fresh coffee
and the sound of a cat's purr.

there are autumn sunrises
and summer sunsets.

there is that moment after a snowfall
where the air is still

and the whole world is perfectly
covered in a soft white blanket.

there are clear blue afternoons
and star-filled midnights.

there is realizing for the first time
that your value has never been

and will never be dependent
on how another feels about you.

you are worthy today.
you will be worthy tomorrow.

protanomaly

there must be some deeply poetic meaning behind being a
child of october who cannot see every hue autumn has to offer.
even though some of its beauty is lost on me, just knowing it
exists is enough to color my soul in the very same shades.

some inevitabilities

you can't please everyone.

not everyone will like you.

people will talk about you behind your back.

there will always be those who doubt you.

these people don't matter in the grand scheme of things.

the sooner you're able to accept this,

the sooner you can live unapologetically.

mythical

some people would sooner watch you burn
than reach out a hand to help pull you from
the fire. it is in those moments that you must
swallow the flames and become a phoenix—
mighty enough to reduce the world to ash.
merciful enough not to.

space

do what you must to protect your own peace,
and never let anyone make you feel guilty for doing so.

permanence

i used to write poetry with a pencil.
it's not that i had commitment issues—
i just needed to know erasing
my mistakes was an option.

but you can't learn from your mistakes
by pretending that they never happened,
so i picked up a pen and, with bold strokes,
began owning all of mine.

be

be brave.
be fearless.
let your imagination
run wild.
the world is what you make it,
not what it makes you.

sense of self

call me idealistic.
call me a daydreamer.
call me starry-eyed.
call me a fool.
call me whatever you'd like.
believe what you want to believe.
it can never change
who i know myself to be.

the final masquerade

tear off the mask
you've hidden behind
for so long. step out
into the sunlight
and let it kiss your skin.
run until you haven't
a single breath left
and take flight.
bathe in moonlight.
paint yourself with starlight.
break free from the world's grip
and become your truest self.
you were always meant to be
your own universe.

Acknowledgments

My lovely wife, amanda – thank you for your endless support, for always being the first person to look over my work, for every deleted comma and added em dash, for writing such a beautiful foreword for this book, and for being my October soulmate every single day of the year.

Ben Eshleman – thank you for creating the gorgeous, hand-and-heart-carved artwork that graces the cover of this book. They say never to judge a book by its cover, but in this case, I disagree, and I can only hope that those who pick this one up find the inside to be just as beautiful as the outside.

You, the reader – I can never thank you enough for inviting my words in, and for being a part of my story. Publishing is so often obsessed with numbers, from social media followers to how many copies a book has sold, and I think amidst all the projections and expectations, it often forgets that behind those numbers are very real human beings, and I am genuinely so grateful for each and every single one of you who have ever been a part of this journey with me.

About the Author

Parker Lee [they/she] is a non-binary trans woman poet and storyteller, as well as author of *coffee days whiskey nights* and *espresso shots & forget-me-nots*. A midwestern transplant, Parker resides in a coastal New Jersey town alongside wife and poetess amanda lovelace (and their three cats), where they can almost always be found not writing when they should be, drinking way too much coffee, and waxing autumnal every single day of the year.

threads:	@itsparkerlee
instagram:	@itsparkerlee
tiktok:	@itsparkerlee
substack:	@itsparkerlee
website:	byparkerlee.com

Now Available

FEATURING A Q&A WITH AMANDA LOVELACE & PARKER LEE

COFFEE
DAYS

WHISKEY
NIGHTS

POEMS BY

PARKER LEE

from Central Avenue Publishing
www.centralavenuepublishing.com

Made in the USA
Middletown, DE
29 October 2023

41427281R00106